the flap pamphlet series

Flood Season

open, read, turn

Flood Season

the flap pamphlet series (No. 28)
Printed and Bound in the United Kingdom

Published by the flap series, 2021
the pamphlet series of flipped eye publishing
All Rights Reserved

Cover Design by Petraski
Series Design © flipped eye publishing, 2010

Author Photo © Philippe Richelet
First Edition
Copyright © Kwaku Darko-Mensah Jnr. 2021

ISBN-13: 978-1-905233-76-2

Flood Season

Kwaku Darko-Mensah Jnr.

To my parents, and to the loving memory of my paternal grandfather

Contents | *Flood Season*

Days to Water

I enter the season of floods with redemptive thoughts
For houses planted in waterways.

A piece of a cloud has broken through my window.

A path clears where my heart should be.
That's no place to put a road.

Cerulean skies exit the foot of my bed, heaving
My mind wells to disorderly heights.

I've slept on hard water,

My things are in the gutter.
The neighbourhoods are awash

With muddy children trying to unstick
Strong cars from the earth.

Sanctuary

Monsoon winds brewed in the afterlife
Have made landfall, concealing daylight.

I've come to see with you in the dark,

The flame you've nursed inside;
Is it the Sun god reclaiming a false night?

Providing us cover from the breached dam?

What snakes through the crack in the wall?
That solitary ray which fills the pot,

And streaks your spot in the bed,

Mapping out for us
The driest places on earth?

Corrective Ripple

I learn to wash off, in communal nights,
Dust, always hovering, inhabiting
The skin tethered to the periphery.

The strays are loud but they're mine,
Fear trips the shadow sometimes,
That too is mine.

The worshippers are fitful,
In temples leaning behind district ruins,
Their notes piercing clean through the night.

The lord is angled up, ascended with foreigners;
The devil casts his lot with the homestead,
Descended from foreigners.

When we speak of good things,
We mustn't point to the sky.

If Wishes Were a Sound Burial

The sunbaked plot behind our house is spotted with hawkers.

They wail about tiger nuts and corn liquor.
Their voices rival the ivory horns we know
From the courts of kings.

I am caught in the delicate act of restraining
Home in clasped hands,
Held to the ear, listening for a way back.

I've made a place for myself,
Solid as land and bread.
This is the house, it does what I need.

Flesh of my flesh how short-lived a sound;

When bone fragments poke out of teak branches,
And flame trees run out of flowers for the drowned,
You remain as you are, a perfect echo.

Kuukua

Ink-dense nights awash in mythic dog barks.
Area boys watch the lights from passing cars
Dazzle like Dubai, eyes growing
Reckless and large with leaving,

Scars in their stomachs outweighing the risk.

Because I love you, Kuukua, I carve myself
Into a dinghy and sail in the mist.
In every version of this dream,
The horizon glimpsed through the bars,

Is a challenge to the permanence of the cage.

In a Seaward Trance

I think about my debut meeting with the sea,
Which happens at the cusp of some magnetic dream.
The craggy side of the coast, empties my life of ghosts,

Rips the scorn off my flesh.

There I'm born and I beg to leave;
A chronic zeal for far-flung beginnings.
Our mother, knower of all things, says I'll one day leave,

And grow sick of leaving.

Spirit Guides

Setting out from the northern edges, where rain is prayed for,
Into the core where it is found threatening,
I am greeted by a gust of ominous city sounds.

I watch a child fetch a ball from the Alajo gutter.
Her friends lower a line,
Their grip the only charter between her skin and the neglect beneath.

Ferried in a stream of peculiar light, drifting along,
A heap of discarded longings brought to the city.
Smell of sewage rises like altar smoke.

Beneath a council of godlike clouds,
Her fate passes from one jurisdiction to another;
A new pantheon takes over.

Ode to Vultures

A convoy of vultures descends on the lagoon.

In swells and breaks of the city's hunting
Match, almost nothing can eat them.

The red dirt is a long enough blanket
For the youth flowing in from the edges.

Sometimes people are driven mad
By their own extraordinary gifts of survival.

Listen:

You can hear muffled screams; there go the vultures,
With generous portions of the country's physiognomy.

Reunion of Pairs

A steel pail of water, black soap splattered hands.
Kneading and turning awakens the bones and mats the hair.

False coat of exile, washed off my skin.
Outside, a hand swipes the wet rim of a mortar.

Pounding rings through the courtyard.
A bucket of water is dumped out of a little window,

Palm fronds slosh across the wet concrete.
A rainbow lizard emerges from a crack in the wall,

Embraces light.
Eyes like twin moons search

The dusk: double nodding.

Birth of the Trickster Spirit

The desert grows restless, trying to meet the sea.
Every time I look back, someone new is in the way,

Someone new is buried,
Everyone's home is in the ground below the trees.

Sea creatures acquire a strange temperament,
Chasing after comfortable water.

There is a hole the size of an earth mound
In the dragnet.

A new sky hangs like a tarp beneath the ancient one.
Every teardrop is blackened water.

I used to breathe beautifully and refuse labour,
Living as life had been in emergence.

A fruit bat colony owned the sky then
And matched the foot traffic in the markets.

What Are We

I take sanctuary in wild, uncharted places,
A creature in grounded worship sneaking up
From a temple of tiger orchids and buffelgrass.

What are we now, that we're in danger?
Cold bodies down, no worlds are strange.

Everyone's hand in the mire,
No nature besides our nature,
Is a mantra worth sustaining;
Symbols can't replicate the unity of our origins.
What are we now?

What are we now, that we're in danger?
Cold bodies down, no worlds are strange.

Rapids of youth erode the riverbed.
A liquid mirror fits a beast head.
The vain want everything except self-recognition
What are we now?

What are we now, that we're in danger?
Cold bodies down, no worlds are strange.
What are we now?

Lifespan of a Grandfather Clock

Frayed at the edges of my mind is a memory of you.
In your hands, a small mirror with a frame of unvarnished wood.
Tufts of hair fall to the sides of the chair you're sat in.
An apron is draped over you.
Papa works a pair of heavy scissors.
Mama is in the doorway flanked by offspring.
The house I visit in this vision,
Isn't the one where there have been ghost sightings,
No.
Not the one with a tannery behind the railway tracks.
But rather the house in which I'd inherited you inside a clock.
A pendulum swinging and clicking at its base.
Your presence swaying it behind a pane of glass.
I watch for when the clock will stop, and time will carry on.

House Sitting for the Spirits

Everywhere the light from the kerosene
Lamp falls, there is a hole: All
My parts laid bare in the midnight deluge,
The pace of change mud slick slow.
An outpour is coming: Entirely up to us
How we decide to stave off despair,
Bargaining the night for smooth passing
Of fast water. Lights out tonight.
Stay and hide from the surge.

Eternity Has No Opposite

From very early on I
Despised this language,
Tongued around it like a fish bone,
Hated how it suggested opposites for everything,
Including eternity;
Hated the condition it imposed on my breathing,
How it implied that stories had a necessary arc,
Then collapsed at the end,
Never to be heard from again ,
When more complicated truths had been curled in other tongues.
I bucked like a wild horse, charged the plains
In search of an archaic pool of wisdom,
To drown jumpy verbs in.
English words crumbling forts in the gut,
Overflowing in sentence,
Flattened by sonorous winds.

Takoradi Polyclinic

I remember when Obi was born, the nurse
Laid his raffia mat, then the priest came
With holy water, said of the boy's eyes,

That they were well aged.

I wish I saw the spirit behind things
As clearly as I see them now,
And sketched the future for him as dense

As the night, begged for songs

To be shared: choral, shrill and haunting songs
To compliment the harvest Sun,
And to let his days ripen with grace.

But I was just then learning

To smoothen and count stones;
What could be said about things hidden in plain sight
That newbirth couldn't untangle.

Sunsum

I have this demand that we make peace with our surroundings. I want thick forests bleeding out of Accra's heart, I want lush gardens to possess the regions. I want them unbounded, in every conceivable direction; I crave that emerald presence, the colour of promises gratified. I want children bathing in sweet crystalline lakes - I want that memory to be all they recall of youth. I want the drizzle on my tongue flavoured like almonds. I want air so pure I'm aroused by breathing.

End the desecration of our water bodies.
Don't you know that god drinks from them?

I want the energies of regression which have heaped spells of decay on homes and fruit trees alike, exorcised. When a funeral procession converges let the reason be death, and death alone – not that a road leading nowhere has committed murder again.

Things Revolutions Couldn't Fix

When we heard the good thing you did,
we cheered and swore by your many names.

In the night we filled craters with water to bathe your feet,
Flames from a lit candle dancing to our melodies of praise.

We danced like the flames, every one of us,
When we heard the good thing, you did.

We danced like the flames. Made ourselves
Into shadows. Every distorted size. Star-possessed.

The dark unable to subdue us.
We danced like the flames.

Horn Player Dirge

It is said that the world ends in fire.
An angel, playing a mean horn, summons with a riff,

A shadowy creature,

To begin reaping from the groove what it hasn't sown.
Future coming at earth's inhabitants as enraged notes,

Ripping holes through empires.

Shells for Shells

We are cleaved by the water and I cannot hear.
A flush of a breaking wave dislodges kin.
I drain the Atlantic out of my ears.
Now and again, I crave release from all that gurgling.
In a refraction of moonlit poise from the same
Heaven that disbands us. Knowing
We'll be as lovely and fluid on land.

Ceremony

I've put on a track of land as generational armour
Against the unfamiliar fit of a new country.

Which hasn't got enough room for my forced wandering
From one end of the world to the other.

What concerns the flesh concerns the spirit;
My folds have grown enormous.

Its weight is lodged in my knees.
It shows in my gait that a thing lives more permanently than refuge.

State Express

I smoked 555's for the road, just like we used to,
In the backseat of a rusty Datsun
With exposed ignition cables, watching police
Openly carry AK 47's
Assembled at Suame Magazine.

Pondering your casual trust for life.
The only successful alchemist I knew. Making verses
Out of excursions nearing death. You said once that It gets lighter,
Considering the fact that we're all just joyriding
Around the sun.

Renewal of a Promise

Invoking a messianic archetype,
At once everyone's and no one's
Ancestor, sets right the path of a faithful seeker.

It may be virtuous to call after the first
Born of everything, but it is not sound
To perceive a likeness of divinity.

Fear No Transit

Whenever I have to fly, I wonder
What the probability is, of not arriving
In one piece. How devastating it'll be
For everyone waiting on me.

Something about being that high up
Makes me feel twice my age. Nights passed
In transit and days rolled out of days. Up
In the air, a jurisdiction in the future.

A city is supposed to be at end of all this suspense.

Somewhat related:

One time a motorcycle missed me by a hair on
Frankfurter Allee. I was ignoring the crosswalk,
thinking about how best to not run out of money. How
did I get out of the way? Felt like a hand picked me
up and placed me onto the safety of the sidewalk. The
motorcyclist had come to a stop, shocked how close
we'd both come to fatal harm. After that brush with
death, I found out the patron saint of travelling poets
had died. All god's children need travelling shoes.
She never lied.

Sermon on a Bus

First, a word of prayer for protection.
The speaker turns the words away from himself.

The origin of danger, which is known,
Will never be acknowledged.

Blessed thieves and dark traps.
They reveal where paved roads end.

Perils worth of plantain and cocoyam
Are strapped to the roof. There are many faces of death,

And they are pressed against the bus windows.
The hands that raised the dead wouldn't turn stones

To bread. Roadblocks appear in place of a rest stop.
The speaker blankets his congregation in thicker coats

Of prayer, counting travelling mercies for the yet to be born.
A screaming baby recoils at the imbalance,

Life and death on opposing wings.

Transplants and Orchards

When your mother asks me at dinner,
As I struggle with a fork and a steak knife,
What people eat where I am from,
Two tongues go to war in my mouth, I subdue one and
Reply, "Cassava, we make everything out of cassava"
She buys it.

In an effort to reclaim home,
I dig holes the size of felled mountains.
Thinking I will plant an orchard of familiar
Fruit trees in full view of the new country.

I think about my Uncle P and his folkloric fall
From a mango tree, and how he could just wait for the fruit to drop.
Instead, he keeps his habit of scaling ambitious heights and ends up all the way
    in Italy.
We are all Uncle P, scaling up a tall tree.

I consider the effortless queuing of worker ants,
In various states of conflict and cooperation;
From the yard of my childhood home,
Into a crack in an open-kitchen cabinet.
As the proverb goes, they are storing crumbs for the winter.
Never mind the relevance of that proverb to our native weather.

In my carefree days, where I belong, I lay on the ground
Absorbing the music of droning flies
Trapped in the screen door,
Trying to extinguish the sun.

My arms, stretched out and parted
Like corn husks to embrace a peripatetic future,
A line running clean through my hair,
A branch on each side.

What will happen to our grandmother's house?
After it's lost grip of the land it is set on?
After we've paid tribute to the last of her brothers
Who put it there?

My heart belongs to the tree that must begin somewhere new.
I've combed my lineage for a word for home
That means more than concrete and dirt.

The Diviner

I attempt to decrypt my fate in a bowl
Of fresh palm nut soup,
And see, to my surprise,
That there really is something there.
Roads have devoured all the potent earth, yet
The places of comfort are never finished.

Never-Ending Dawn

A melody is flowering within you,
The synchronous day rests its naked face in your lap,
Your body at ease in hints of dawn.
Could it be the trick of loose tongues?
Balancing calm and sweet chaos inside
Chaos, an organising principle.
Everything is everything it will become.

Area Gods

Desiring more than this nation can feed,
We turn the average night into a parade:
Part church, part protest.

The wooden shack bars glow dirty orange
From longings unmuted.
A carnival of sleepless dreamers,

We study each other to the music.
So many paths in this universe,
You could go in one way and come out another.

Ancestral Time

I witnessed a European tourist have a seizure in one of the dungeons at Cape Coast castle just as a band of Fanti priests were in the middle of an atoning ritual. Her companion said it was a heat stroke; her eyes rolled into the back of her head, arms flailing like a malfunctioning compass. It was hot that day, but not any hotter than it had been for the past 100 years. The horizon stretched far beyond a single point of view. Ancestral time is always and forever now

After the Storm

High over kaleidoscopic stalls lodged into caked earth,
Starlings in flight;
A benevolent sky hovers over far-out grass fields,
Sunlight punctured.
Specs of gold adorn the edge of a new season,
The moist earth grows something good in its belly.

Exiled Poets' Society

Many of our exiles left impossible shoes to fill,
The state kept ruining their inheritance with its death throes,
But these days poets don't leave like they used to,
They multiply.

Auto

Let's make sunsets loop
Between our lips,
Dazzling in a forever dream

Designed for the gods to envy
How perfectly our parts fit.
To crave deathlessness and be fully aware of it;

With you, no loss is threatening
Not even here, where bridges collapse and
Water is just a prelude to our vastness.

Omni

The future will not be
Decked out in jewels of data,
Safe from casual cruelty,
Where all things sublime no longer threaten us.

It will not ease the instinct for starting fires
While asking, "if this is heaven why do we burn?"
Or knot a snake by its tail
After it has died calmly in its sleep, or
Trade lead for oxygen, 85 cents a breath.

It will not harvest labour in Africa,
Shackle it in the belly of an alien ship,
Trap it between centuries,
To be reborn on cold earth,
To be possessed by the cotton gin.

It will not speak highly of the sea,
How it's ruffled our home against the memory of you,
Which it separates from me.
It will not light a cryptic text
On an impatient dreamer's screen asking,
"…if not now then… now?"

It will not blame the weather for what it lacks in its soul,
Or a higher intelligence forged in its image.

Days From Water

The pulse of the day slows and the people I know who
Sell things pack it in 'til after the rains.

The last chorus of a work song is drowned out
By the sound of waves splashing a nude coast.

Every year, the boys go to sea returning
With ever decreasing stock & clenched fists.

Kerosene lamps glow orange in an unlit republic,
The smell of smoked tilapia & herring blanket Jamestown.

Old slave forts have begun their surrender to the sea &
Look what time has done to everything it's trapped -

Night from day, morning from decay.